CELEBRATING
VALENTINE'S
DAY

BY ANN HEINRICHS · ILLUSTRATED BY SHARON HOLM

The Child's World®
childsworld.com

Published by The Child's World®
1980 Lookout Drive • Mankato, MN 56003-1705
800-599-READ • www.childsworld.com

ISBN 9781503853911 (Reinforced Library Binding)
ISBN 9781503854772 (Portable Document Format)
ISBN 9781503855151 (Online Multi-user eBook)
LCCN: 2021930083

Printed in the United States of America

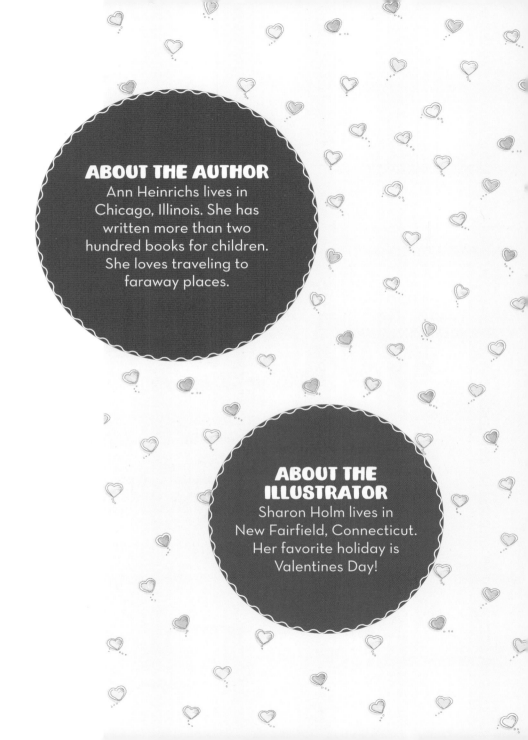

ABOUT THE AUTHOR
Ann Heinrichs lives in Chicago, Illinois. She has written more than two hundred books for children. She loves traveling to faraway places.

ABOUT THE ILLUSTRATOR
Sharon Holm lives in New Fairfield, Connecticut. Her favorite holiday is Valentines Day!

CONTENTS

Happy Valentine's Day!

Bright red hearts are everywhere. People give each other pretty cards. Gifts of flowers and candy bring warm smiles. It's Valentine's Day!

Valentine's Day is a happy holiday. It celebrates love and friendship. What's the best greeting for Valentine's Day? Tell someone "I love you." Or just say, "You are special!"

Roses are red,
Violets are blue,
If you'll be my sweetheart,
I'll be yours, too!

Valentine's Day is a time to celebrate love and friendship.

Aiming for the Heart

A VALENTINE

Go, Cupid, and my sweetheart tell
I love her well.
Yes, though she tramples on my heart
And rends that bleeding thing apart;
And though she rolls a scornful eye
On doting me when I go by;
And though she scouts at everything
As tribute unto her I bring—
Apple, banana, caramel—
Haste, Cupid, to my love and tell,
In spite of all, I love her well!

—Eugene Field (1850-1895)

Many **ancient** peoples had a god of love. For ancient Romans, it was Cupid. Cupid appears as a baby with wings. He carries a bow and arrow. What does he aim for? People's hearts! Whoever is shot falls in love.

Have you seen valentines showing flying babies? They're not angels. They're little Cupids!

Cupid is a
knavish **lad**,
**Thus to make poor
females mad.**
—*William Shakespeare
(1564–1616)*

*Ancient Romans believed
Cupid's arrows caused
people to fall in love.*

Choosing Sweethearts

How did Valentine's Day begin? The story goes back more than two thousand years.

Ancient Romans held a festival on February 15. It was called Lupercalia (loo-pur-KAY-lee-uh). Spring was coming soon. It was a time to celebrate new life.

Lupercalia was held shortly before the arrival of spring.

Ancient Romans drew names from a jar to find out who their sweetheart would be.

A special ceremony was held the day before Lupercalia. Girls' names were written on slips of paper. Then they were put into a jar. Each young man drew a girl's name from the jar. The two would be sweethearts during the festival.

In time, the Romans became Christians. They laid aside their old ways. But they would soon have a new holiday for sweethearts.

'Tis better to have loved and lost, Than never to have loved at all.
—Alfred Lord Tennyson (1809-1892)

Who Was
Saint Valentine?

Valentine's Day is often called Saint Valentine's Day. But who was Saint Valentine? Many **legends** are told about him. One says he was a Christian priest in ancient Rome.

The Roman emperor was building up an army. But married men didn't want to join. They wanted to stay home with their wives. So the emperor outlawed marriage.

There are many legends about Saint Valentine.

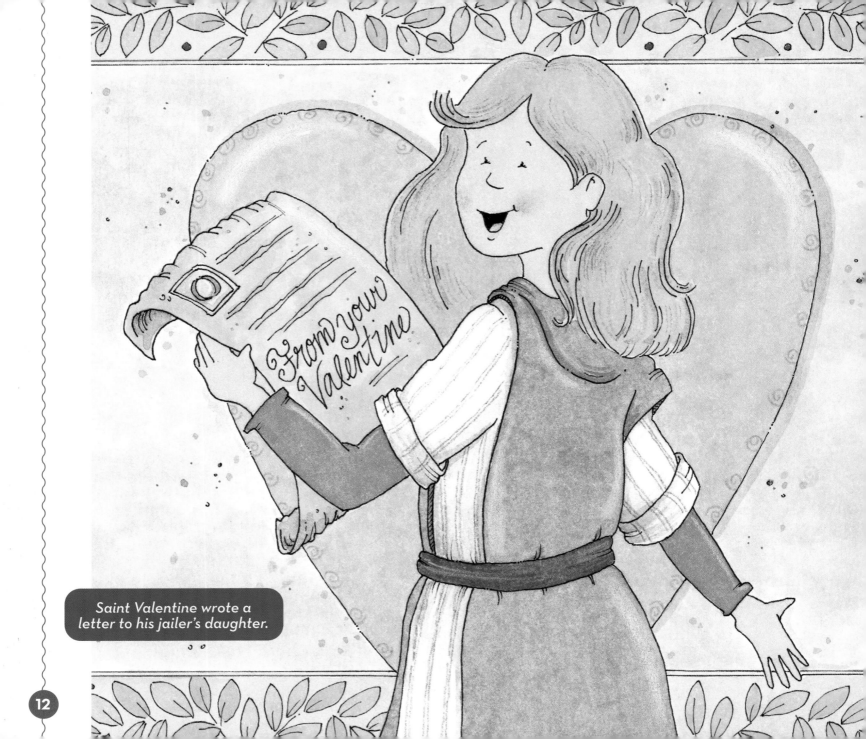

Saint Valentine wrote a letter to his jailer's daughter.

Valentine took pity on couples in love. He secretly married them. But his secret was discovered. He was thrown in jail and sentenced to death.

While in jail, he made friends with the jailer's daughter. Before his death, he sent her a good-bye note. He signed it, "From your Valentine."

Valentine was declared a Christian saint. He became the **patron saint** of people in love. It's said that he died on February 14. So that became Saint Valentine's Day.

A Holiday for Love

Saint Valentine's Day became a popular holiday. It was a day to celebrate love!

One Valentine's Day custom arose in England and Scotland. Young people put their names in a bowl. Then they drew names to see who their sweetheart would be. They wore the name on their sleeve.

Girls in England had another custom. A girl thought of all the boys she liked. She wrote each one's name on a piece of paper. She rolled each paper up in a ball of clay. Then she put the clay balls in a jar of water. The first name that rose to the top would be her valentine!

Who I am I shall not say,
But I send you this bouquet
With this **query**, baby mine:
"Will you be my valentine?"
—*Eugene Field*
(1850–1895)

A number of Valentine's Day games began in England and Scotland.

Oh, if it be to choose and call thee mine, Love, thou art every day my Valentine!
—Thomas Hood (1799–1845)

Who Will Be My Valentine?

Many beliefs arose about Saint Valentine's Day. One was that birds chose their mates on February 14. So people believed that they should do the same!

Girls rushed to their windows that morning. They believed the first person they saw would be their valentine. Some girls left nothing to chance. They stood at their sweetheart's window!

A young woman watched for birds that day, too. Was a robin flying overhead? That meant she'd marry a sailor. Did she see a sparrow? Then she would marry a poor man. What if she saw a goldfinch? She would marry a rich man!

Tomorrow is Saint Valentine's day,
All in the morning **betime**,
And I a maid at your window,
To be your Valentine.
—*William Shakespeare (1564–1616)*

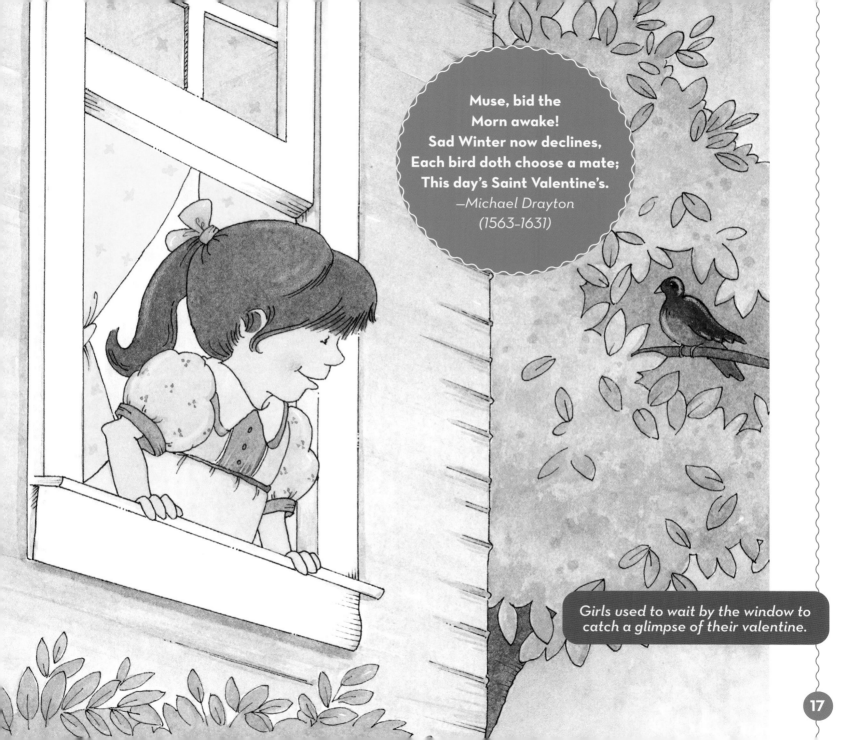

Muse, bid the
Morn awake!
Sad Winter now declines,
Each bird doth choose a mate;
This day's Saint Valentine's.
—*Michael Drayton*
(1563–1631)

Girls used to wait by the window to catch a glimpse of their valentine.

CHAPTER 7
Symbols of Love

Saint Valentine's Day became a day to write love letters. They were often written as poems. The love notes were called valentines. Young men even proposed marriage in valentines.

By the 1700s, there were valentines for sale. They were beautiful! They were trimmed with lace, silk, and ribbons. Feathers and flowers were attached. Even drops of perfume were added.

These valentines showed many **symbols** of love. We still see them on valentines today. Bright red hearts are favorites. An arrow often pierces the heart. Who shoots the arrow? Little Cupid, the god of love!

A hundred years
would be too few
To carry all my love for you.
—Author unknown

Doves are a symbol of eternal love.

Be joy for ever

Pairs of doves are another symbol. They stand for **eternal** love. Why? Because doves mate for life. Doves also make cooing sounds—like sweethearts do!

Love looks
not with the eyes,
but with the mind,
And therefore is winged
Cupid painted blind.
—*William Shakespeare
(1564–1616)*

Celebrating Love and Friendship

People still like giving valentines. Sweethearts give each other cards. Parents, teachers, and classmates give them, too. Valentines are also a good way to tell friends they're special.

Flowers are popular Valentine's Day gifts. Red roses are favorites. They stand for a loving heart.

Many people give gifts of candy. Children like little heart-shaped candies. Other people give chocolates. Either way, the message is clear. Candy means "You are sweet!"

At the touch of love, everyone becomes a poet.
—Plato
(428-348 BC)

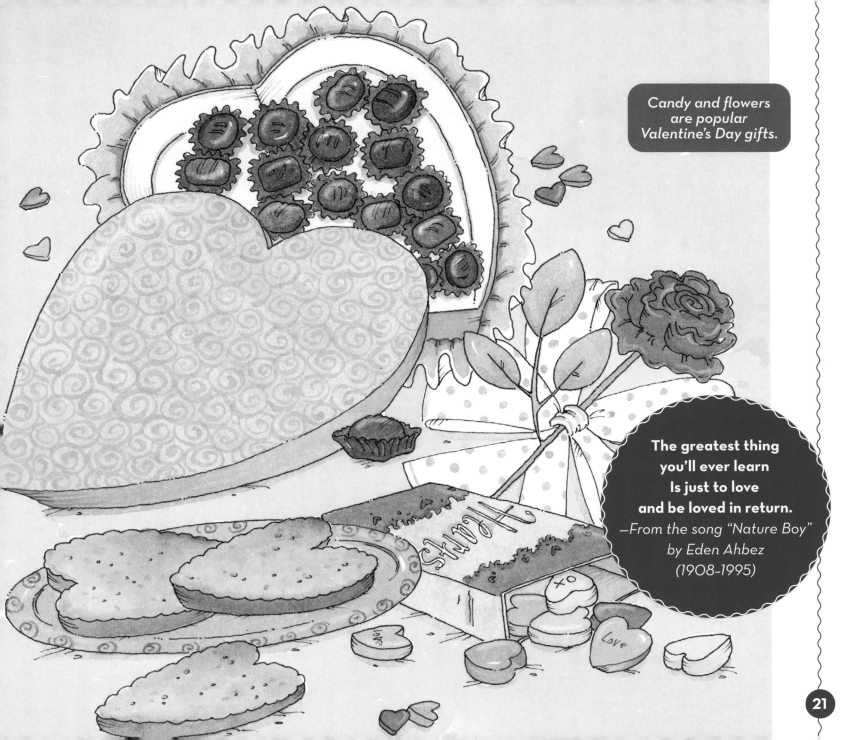

Candy and flowers are popular Valentine's Day gifts.

The greatest thing you'll ever learn Is just to love and be loved in return.
—From the song "Nature Boy" by Eden Ahbez (1908–1995)

Poetry Corner

WILL YOU BE MY VALENTINE?

Will you be my Valentine?
I know that I am yours.
You are like a tossing sea
And I am like your shores.

You are like an endless wave
And I your waiting sand,
And I will wait forever as
You come and smooth my hand.

I will wait forever, yet
You are a part of me.
I hold you in my arms, while you
Come to me endlessly.

Will you be my Valentine?
I know that I am yours.
I love you with a love that yearns
To be your golden shores.

—*Author unknown*

AN ANSWER TO A VALENTINE

My true love sent me
a valentine
All on a winter's day,
And suddenly the cold gray skies
Grew soft and warm as May!

The snowflakes changed
to apple blooms,
A pink-white fluttering crowd,
And on the swaying
maple boughs
The robins sang aloud. . . .
O love of mine, my Valentine!
This is no winter day—
For Love rules all the calendars,
And Love knows only May!

—*Julia Caroline Ripley Dorr (1825–1913)*

JOINING IN THE SPIRIT OF VALENTINE'S DAY

* Make a special Valentine's Day card for a favorite relative. It could be for a brother, sister, parent, grandparent, uncle, or aunt.

* Think of words that rhyme with "love." Then write a Valentine's Day poem. End each line with a rhyming word.

* Is there a home for older people in your community? Visit them on Valentine's Day. Bring cheery cards and flowers. Ask them about their younger days.

* Do you know someone from another country? Ask if his or her country has a special holiday for sweethearts.

MAKING QUEEN OF HEARTS TARTS

What you need:
2 1/4 cups all-purpose flour
2 teaspoons baking powder
1/4 teaspoon salt
1/2 cup shortening
1 cup sugar
2 eggs
1/2 teaspoon vanilla
1 tablespoon milk
2 jars of strawberry or raspberry jam

Directions

1. Preheat the oven to 375 degrees Fahrenheit.*

2. Mix the flour, baking powder, and salt in a large bowl.

3. In a separate bowl, stir together the shortening and sugar. Pour this creamy mixture into the first bowl, and add eggs, vanilla, and milk. Mix well.

4. Sprinkle a little flour onto a baking board or other flat, clean surface. Pour the mixture on this surface.

5. Use a heart-shaped cookie cutter to cut the dough into about fifty pieces.

6. Place the hearts on a cookie sheet and bake for eight to ten minutes.

7. Cool for about thirty minutes.

8. Once cool, spread jam on each cookie with a plastic knife and top with another cookie.

*Have an adult help you operate the oven.

MAKING A VALENTINE CARD SCRAPBOOK

What you need:
2 pieces of red or pink construction paper
10 pieces of plain white paper
Yarn or string
A ruler
A hole punch
Markers, crayons, stickers, and glitter for decorating
Scissors
Glue

Directions

1. Decorate both pieces of construction paper with Valentine's Day pictures such as hearts, candy, and cupids. On the piece that will be the front cover, you may want to write "Valentine's Day," the year, and your name.

2. Place the ten sheets of plain white paper in between the two decorated pieces of construction paper. Be sure that the piece you decorated as the front cover is on top. The back cover sheet should be on the bottom with the decorated side facing out.

3. Use the hole punch to punch three holes through the side of the stack of paper. One hole should be near the top, one in the middle, and one near the bottom. Ask an adult for help if it is hard to punch through all of the sheets at once.

4. Cut three 5-inch pieces of yarn or string.

5. Put one 5-inch piece of string through the top set of holes and tie a double knot. If you would like, tie the string in a bow.

Now you have a scrapbook ready to hold all of your valentines!

GLOSSARY

ancient (AYN-shunt)—very old; often meaning thousands of years old

betime (bee-TYME)—old word for "early"

eternal (ee-TUR-null)—never-ending

knavish (NAY-vish)—tricky or deceptive

legends (LEJ-undz)—tales from the past

patron saint (PAY-trun SAYNT)—a holy person with special meaning to a group of people

query (KWEER-ee)—a question

scouts (SKAOWTS)—old word for "mocks" or "rejects"

symbols (SIM-bullz)—objects, images, or words that stand for an idea

LEARN MORE

BOOKS

Brevard, Bethany. *The Mouse in the Hammock: A Valentine's Tale*. Austin, TX: Dream Big Publishing, 2021.

Elliot, Rob. *Laugh-Out-Loud Valentine's Day Jokes for Kids*. New York, NY: HarperCollins Children's Books, 2021.

Mathiowetz, Claire. *Valentine's Day Crafts*. Mankato, MN: The Child's World, 2017.

Otto, Carolyn. *Celebrate Valentine's Day: With Love, Cards, and Candy*. Washington, DC: National Geographic, 2016.

Suen, Anastasia. *Valentine's Day Gifts*. Vero Beach, FL: Rourke, 2018.

WEBSITES

Visit our website for links about Valentine's Day and other holidays:
childsworld.com/links

Note to Parents, Teachers, and Librarians: We routinely verify our Web links to make sure they are safe and active sites. So encourage your readers to check them out!

INDEX